IMAGES
of America

THE UNITED STATES
NAVAL ACADEMY

IMAGES
of America

THE UNITED STATES NAVAL ACADEMY

Lt. Christopher G. Miller, USN (Ret.)

ARCADIA
PUBLISHING

Published by Arcadia Publishing
Charleston, South Carolina

Printed in the United States of America

Library of Congress Control Number: 2023942372

For all general information, please contact Arcadia Publishing:
Telephone 843-853-2070
Fax 843-853-0044
E-mail sales@arcadiapublishing.com

Visit us on the Internet at www.arcadiapublishing.com

For James.

CONTENTS

ACKNOWLEDGMENTS

I spent three years teaching English at the Naval Academy, and that outstanding experience is what inspired this book. While all the photographs in the book are in the public domain, they would not be available without the team at the Nimitz Library Special Collections Department at the US Naval Academy. The library staff's dedication to preserving the history of one of the finest academic institutions in the world is impressive. I would also like to thank my Coast Guard family at Education & Training Quota Management Command in Norfolk, Virginia. Finally, I would like to thank my husband, James, for his unwavering support.

INTRODUCTION

The US Navy was born during the American Revolution, when the need for a naval force to match the Royal Navy became clear. But during the period immediately following the Revolution, the Continental Navy was demobilized in 1785 by an economy-minded Congress. This dormancy lasted barely a decade when, in 1794, Pres. George Washington persuaded Congress to authorize a new naval force to combat the growing menace of piracy on the high seas.

The first vessels of the new US Navy were launched in 1797; among them were the *United States*, the *Constellation*, and the *Constitution*. These first ships would later play a role in training midshipmen in Annapolis. In 1825, Pres. John Quincy Adams urged Congress to establish the Naval Academy "for the formation of scientific and accomplished officers." His proposal, however, was not acted upon until 20 years later.

When the founders of the US Naval Academy (USNA) were looking for a suitable location, it was reported that then secretary of the Navy George Bancroft decided to place the naval school in "the healthy and secluded" area of Annapolis, Maryland, to rescue midshipmen from "the temptations and distractions that necessarily connect with a large and populous city" like Philadelphia, Boston, or New York.

Through the efforts of Secretary Bancroft, the Naval School was established without Congressional funding at a 10-acre Army post named Fort Severn in Annapolis on October 10, 1845, with a class of 50 midshipmen and seven professors. The curriculum included mathematics, navigation, gunnery and steam, chemistry, English, natural philosophy, and French.

In 1850, the Naval School became the US Naval Academy. A new curriculum required midshipmen to study at the academy for four years and train aboard ships each summer. That format is the basis of a far more advanced and sophisticated curriculum at the Naval Academy today. As the US Navy grew over the years, the academy expanded. The campus of 10 acres increased to 338. The original student body of 50 midshipmen has grown to a brigade size of 4,000. Modern granite buildings replaced the old wooden structures of Fort Severn.

Congress authorized the Naval Academy to award bachelor of science degrees in 1933. The academy later replaced a fixed curriculum taken by all midshipmen with the current core curriculum plus 18 major fields of study, a wide variety of elective courses, and advanced study and research opportunities.

Since then, the development of the US Naval Academy has reflected the country's history. As America has changed culturally and technologically, so has the Naval Academy. In just a few decades, the Navy moved from a fleet of sail and steam-powered ships to a high-tech fleet with supersonic aircraft, submarines, and surface ships, many of them nuclear-powered. The academy has changed, too, giving midshipmen the state-of-the-art academic and professional training they need to be effective naval officers in their future careers.

The Naval Academy first accepted women as midshipmen in 1976, when Congress authorized the admission of women to all of the service academies. Women comprise over 20 percent of entering plebes—or freshmen—and they pursue the same academic and professional training as their male classmates.

Author Note: The United States Naval Academy has many stories to tell. The photographs in this book tell just one of them. The vast majority of the images in this book predate what could be called the modern era of the Naval Academy (1976-present). I also wanted to note that the photographs do not appear in any particular order within their respective chapters.

One

BUILDINGS, GROUNDS, BOATS, AND SHIPS

This drawing shows the grounds and buildings that made up the Naval Academy, sometimes called "The Yard," in the early 20th century. The small type at the top and bottom of the image notes essential elements of the campus, such as officer houses, physics and campus buildings, steam engineering, and the Severn River.

This vintage postcard shows the grounds and buildings that made up the Naval Academy in the 1930s. Several wings had been added to Bancroft Hall since the image on the previous page was made. The postcard also clearly shows the Naval Academy Bridge at top.

Bancroft Hall, U. S. Naval Academy,
Annapolis, Md.

This 1900 photograph shows a rear view of Bancroft Hall, the historical midshipmen's residence. The class of 1900 had 61 graduates, so approximately 250 young men called this building home. Bancroft Hall is the largest academic dormitory in America, with over 1,700 rooms.

Academic Hall, Annapolis, Md.

Academic Hall is on the public-facing side of Bancroft Hall. Each day at lunchtime, the Brigade of Midshipmen musters in front of the hall, receives their daily instruction, and reports to King Hall for lunch and some camaraderie. Visitors can enter the building after the demonstration and view a mock-up of the average midshipmen dorm room and other exhibits.

Mahan Hall is one of the original academic buildings designed by Ernest Flagg. Initially, it included a library and auditorium. The latter is still in use for theater productions. The academy now has a separate, much more extensive library. The building also included the rear-facing Isherwood Hall marine engineering building, which was demolished in the early 1980s to provide space for Alumni Hall, the campus arena. The building is flanked by Sampson and Maury Halls, which house the liberal arts classrooms. The building was named for Alfred Thayer Mahan, the well-known naval historian and strategist who wrote *The Influence of Sea Power Upon History*, a must-read for any maritime officer. Maury Hall was renamed in honor of Pres. Jimmy Carter in February 2023.

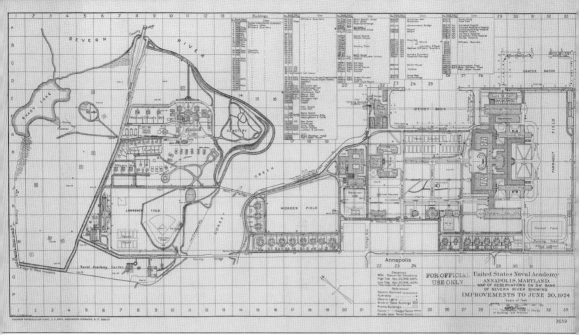

The most recent addition to this US Naval Academy Improvements detailed map would have been Luce Hall, completed in 1920. At the top of the map, numerous plots have been set aside for future expansion. The open area on the left (north) side of the map is predominantly military housing today. It also includes the Navy Exchange and Commissary and the ice hockey rink. Worden Field, at center, was the original home of the academy football team. It now hosts drills and parades and is much smaller than depicted here.

Naval Engineering Experiment Station,
U.S.Naval Academy,
Annapolis, Md.

Conceived by Adm. George Melville, the noted Arctic explorer, the Naval Engineering Experiment Station has been a critical part of the Yard for over 100 years. It includes six laboratories (three original) that help test new equipment for the Navy before it is sent to shipyards for installation on ships. This was necessary because Congress passed a law in 1861 requiring any equipment for ships to be tested before installation. Initially, the station worked in conjunction with the engineering department at the academy, but it now runs independently. Midshipmen spend time in the laboratory as it relates to their studies.

ADMINISTRATION BUILDING, U. S. NAVAL ACADEMY, ANNAPOLIS, MD.

The administration building, now known as Larson Hall, was built in 1907 and renovated in 2014. It houses the superintendent and the administrative support staff of the academy. It was renamed in 2015 for Adm. Charles Larson, who served as the superintendent twice, from 1983 to 1986 and 1994 to 1998. He is buried at the Naval Academy Cemetery next to his best friend, Sen. John McCain. The building has undergone several refurbishments but still retains its historical architecture.

THE NAVAL ACADEMY—SIDE VIEW.

This is a wood engraving taken from a drawing by W.R. Miller published in the *Illustrated News* in March 1853. None of the buildings depicted here remain on the grounds. The building at center is the old Fort Severn, built in 1808. It and two additional parcels of land were purchased from the US Army in 1845 for the future Naval Academy. The fort was in use on the grounds until 1909.

These are two parts of a panoramic northwest view of Bancroft, Dahlgren, and MacDonough Halls. The Naval Academy Chapel is also visible, so the photograph dates from at least 1908. A large sailing vessel can be seen at far right. Retired ships have often played a part in the training and education of midshipmen.

This brick path, known as Stribling Walk, leads directly from Bancroft Hall to the academic buildings. It is named for Rear Adm. Cornelius Stribling, a leader during the War of 1812, the Barbary Wars, the Mexican-American War, and the Civil War. Legend has it that the original path had 11,880 bricks to mark the year of his death, 1880. This winter photograph is relatively modern, given the presence of the academic buildings at right.

This 1896 stereograph by noted photographer Alfred Campbell of Elizabeth, New Jersey, would have been included in a group of similar images sold as a set. The two-dimensional image would have appeared three-dimensional when viewed through a stereoscope. Several individuals are present, along with quite a few cannons. Stereographs were popular in the latter half of the 19th century because they were affordable and reached across class lines.

The New Quarters was designed and hastily built during Rear Adm. David D. Porter's superintendency. The Brigade of Midshipmen would line up for formation along the walkway in front for inspections, meal formations, classes, parades, and graduation ceremonies. These quarters were deemed necessary after the expanded Brigade of Midshipmen returned from Newport, Rhode Island, after the Civil War. The building, pictured here in the 1880s, was replaced by Bancroft Hall after only 40 years.

This photograph was taken during the first meeting of the US Naval Institute in 1871. The conference of 15 officers took place on the second floor of the lecture hall (center foreground). The original physics and chemistry buildings are pictured, and the school ships *Constitution*, *Santee*, *Marion*, and *Dale* are moored to the piers at right. A steamship is also moored at Phlox Wharf.

MacDonough (pictured) and Dahlgren Halls are virtually identical buildings that flank Bancroft Hall. Although their uses have changed, both buildings remain largely intact. They were among the first of Ernest Flagg's facilities to be completed and, unlike several others in his Beaux-Arts complex, were built almost exactly as he envisioned. MacDonough Hall is now a premier gymnastics facility. The men's and women's teams are both members of the Eastern College Athletic Conference (ECAC).

The interior of Dahlgren Hall is pictured as it would have appeared after construction. Several cannons are on display. Small arms and rifles are to the left and right. An extensive collection of swords is proudly displayed on the rear wall. This building was used for graduation from 1903 to 1957. From 1975 to 2006, it housed the academy ice rink. The midshipmen now have a standalone ice rink at the McMullen Hockey Arena on the other side of the Severn River.

The Naval Academy Bridge crossed the Severn River and served Annapolis and the academy from 1924 to 1994. It was made of concrete and had a low-level steel drawbridge. It was also known for a time as the College Creek Bridge.

The Fitch footbridge crosses Dorsey Creek and connects the main campus with Forest Sherman Field. It is common to see hundreds of people crossing the bridge after a parade at the field or during graduation festivities.

The US Naval Postgraduate School had its origin in 1909, when the developing need for specialized training of naval officers led to the School of Marine Engineering being established as part of the academy. In 1912, it became the Postgraduate Department of the Naval Academy, and the curriculum was broadened. In 1921, the name Postgraduate School was adopted. The school extended its fields of study, accepted officers from other services, and established the Naval Intelligence School at Anacostia in Washington, DC, and the General Line School (covering professional subjects) at Newport, Rhode Island, while the graduate engineering school was retained in Annapolis. In 1947, the school was separated from the Naval Academy, given authority to grant master's and doctorate degrees, received Congressional approval for a branch at Monterey, California, and became officially known as the US Naval Postgraduate School.

The Atlantic House, a summer hotel on the corner of Pelham and Touro Streets in Newport, housed the US Naval Academy during the Civil War. The US Navy chose to protect it and its students from Confederate forces because of the vulnerable location of Annapolis. After the war, the Navy appreciated the strategic location of Newport and returned to build the Naval War College, Torpedo Station, and Training Station here. Naval Station Newport is also home to the Naval Academy Preparatory School today. Interestingly, no significant engagements took place in Annapolis during the war.

The Ishwerwood buildings are pictured as they appeared before being demolished to make room for Alumni Hall. Isherwood Hall was constructed in 1905 and was home to the Department of Marine Engineering.

This indoor arena, Alumni Hall, was built in 1991 and serves as the primary meeting space when the entire brigade needs to be together. It seats almost 6,000 people. It is also home to Navy men's basketball. In the early summer, it serves as the starting point for plebes on their journey to become midshipmen. Plebes disembark from busses, say goodbye to their parents, and stop at several checkpoints within the building, picking up parts of their new life along the way.

This early-20th-century photograph shows midshipmen practicing their tennis skills. The academy has both men's and women's NCAA tennis teams. Additionally, the brigade holds open-court practices and brigade-level tournaments. New courts for the varsity teams are located at the Brigade Sports Complex across the river.

Also known as the "Boat House," Hubbard Hall is the home of the Naval Academy rowing teams. It was constructed in 1930 on Dorsey Creek, a small tributary of the Severn River. The building underwent a $20-million renovation in 2012 to help support the men's and women's teams. It is named after Rear Adm. John Hubbard (USNA 1870), who led the men's team to victory in his senior year. The structure includes a rowing tank, racks for boat storage, a common room, strength conditioning facilities, and an area to maintain the boats.

This beautiful terrace is named for Rear Adm. Benjamin Isherwood, one of the founders of the Navy's Bureau of Steam Engineering. He was also the engineer in chief of the US Navy during the Civil War. He has been honored several times by the Navy, including having a building named for him, Isherwood Hall, which was razed in 1982 to make room for Alumni Hall.

Designed by Ernest Flagg and constructed in 1908, this chapel serves as the primary congregation space for Protestant and Catholic services. It has been through several renovations, with one major renovation in the 1940s adding additional seats to accommodate the expanding Brigade of Midshipmen. This addition created a cross shape. Next to Bancroft Hall, it is the most visited structure at the academy. The chapel was designated a national historic landmark in 1961.

Brilliant light floods the chapel through the multitude of hand-crafted stained-glass windows. Midshipmen, dressed in their summer white uniforms, fill the seats on the left and right. The chapel includes a spectacular pipe organ with 522 draw knobs, a world record. From 1853 to 1972, attendance at Sunday services was mandatory. The crypt of John Paul Jones, father of the American Navy, lies below the chapel.

The academy's Jewish center is named in honor of Commodore Uriah P. Levy (1792–1862), the first Jewish commodore in the US Navy. He refused to impose corporal punishment on his sailors, a common practice throughout the Navy. The building contains a synagogue, learning center, fellowship hall, and several administrative offices for the brigade. The exterior is made of Jerusalem stone. The Levy Center was made possible by the fund-raising efforts of the Friends of the Jewish Chapel, a nonprofit group dedicated to the cultural and spiritual lives of Jewish midshipmen.

The Brigade Synagogue seats over 400. Visitors to the Levy Center and the synagogue might notice similarities to Thomas Jefferson's Monticello. Interestingly, Uriah P. Levy purchased Monticello in 1834 because he admired Jefferson. The architect of the Levy Center, Joseph Boggs, sought to pay tribute to that connection. The interior includes a 45-foot-high replica of the Wailing Wall in Jerusalem.

Griffin Hall was built in 1917 as an extension of Isherwood Hall. Griffin was a skinny rectangle (56 feet by 181 feet) connected at its center by a two-story extension to the southwest side of Isherwood. No significant research or technological discoveries have occurred in the building. However, it did serve as the periodical and bound journals library until Nimitz Library was constructed in 1975. Griffin Hall was named for Rear Adm. Robert S. Griffin (USNA, 1878), a mechanical engineer and chief of the Bureau of Steam Engineering for the US Navy.

Comdr. James Ward was the first US Navy officer killed during the Civil War and was also the first commandant of midshipmen in 1845. Ward Hall now serves as the USNA Information Technology Center.

Before the Nimitz Library (pictured here) opened in 1975, library services were spread throughout the Yard. The library houses the Special Collection and Archives Division, where most of the photographs in this book were sourced. Rickover Hall, built at the same time as Nimitz Library, can be seen in the background. The library is named for Fleet Adm. Chester W. Nimitz (USNA, 1905), who served with distinction from 1905 until his death in 1966. The rank of fleet admiral is a lifetime appointment, so he was on active duty from 1947 until his death even though he was not in active service. A bust of Nimitz greets midshipmen each time they enter the library, reminding them of his importance to the history of the Navy and the Naval Academy.

Preble Hall houses the US Naval Academy Museum, one of the buildings most visited on the Yard and one of only nine official US Navy museums. The museum offers two floors of exhibits about the history of sea power, the development of the US Navy, and the role of the US Naval Academy in producing officers capable of leading America's sailors and marines. The displays combine historical artifacts with video and audio technology to bring to life the stories of the men and women who have served their country at sea.

The first storage area for the academy's cannons, guns, and ammunition was the Laboratory and Philosophical Hall, built in 1854 adjacent to Fort Severn. That building was allotted to the academy's pay and store officer in 1865. A new armory, whose interior is seen here, was built as part of Superintendent David Porter's reconstruction program. The wooden structure was in the rear of the Old Quarters and the Officer's Mess and Quarters on Stribling Row. It was used until 1881, when Congress appropriated $25,000 to construct a third armory building 100 yards northwest of the New Quarters. In 1899, ground was broken on the academy's fourth armory, Dahlgren Hall, which was the first of the new buildings constructed by architect Ernest Flagg, in 1903. The guns at center are Dahlgren boat howitzers.

The first meeting of the US Naval Institute (USNI) occurred here in October 1885. Originally, this building, which dated to 1854, was used as a gunnery room. It was turned over to the newly established USNI in 1885 after being used as a lyceum for two decades. The institute prides itself on being a place for open and independent thought for US Navy, Marine Corps, and Coast Guard personnel. They now have a much larger facility near the cemetery.

Launched in 1862, USS *Monongahela*'s primary mission was to support the US Navy in its blockade of Confederate forces during the Civil War. From 1894 to 1899, she served as a practice ship for the Naval Academy, often taking extended cruises to help train future naval officers. After her service with the academy, she was transferred to Newport to conduct more training.

Named for the father of the nuclear Navy, Adm. Hyman G. Rickover (USNA, 1922), Rickover Hall is the home of the Department of Navy Architecture and Ocean Engineering. Rickover served on active duty from 1918 to 1982. He held a flag rank for most of his career, from 1953 to 1982. This makes him the longest-serving member of the military in American history. Rickover established himself as an early proponent of nuclear power, participating in and overseeing the development of the first pressurized water reactor. This success gave him incredible oversight power of the program for the next 40 years. During his tenure, he personally interviewed every candidate for the Navy's nuclear propulsion program. He was known for his unusual interview style.

This photograph, looking southwest toward the old east gate, features the library and superintendent's office on the left and the second chapel on the right. Posing in front of the shady lane are William H. Wilcox (in uniform), professor of mathematics and head of the Department of Mathematics for more than 15 years, and Thomas Karney, English and ethics professor from 1851 to 1872 and librarian from 1872 to 1885. The three young girls are possibly daughters of Wilcox.

The US Navy has long understood that knowledge, confidence, and respect for the sea instilled through sailing help to make better naval officers. Sailing opportunities at the academy range from basic sail training given during the summer to every incoming plebe, Command & Seamanship Training Squadron during summer training, and the pinnacle of the sport, the varsity intercollegiate and offshore teams. The Robert Crown Center houses administrative and coaching offices, team classrooms, locker rooms, equipment repair, and storage facilities. The center also houses the Intercollegiate Yacht Racing Association Hall of Fame, with exhibits representing 70 years of intercollegiate sailing. Adjacent to Crown Center is Santee Basin, the mooring area for the Naval Academy's 250-plus sail training fleet, including 20 Navy 44s, 6 offshore boats, 12 J-24s, 22 420s, 22 FJs, and 136 Lasers. Practices and races take place on the Severn River and Chesapeake Bay.

INTERIOR BANCROFT HALL, U. S. NAVAL ACADEMY, ANNAPOLIS, MD.

This area of Bancroft Hall is now known as the Rotunda and is open to visitors. It has wings on each side and a large mural on the ceiling that depicts USS *South Dakota* in action during the Battle of the Santa Cruz Islands in World War II. A mockup of a typical midshipman's dorm room is also available for viewing by visitors. The steps at the center of the Rotunda lead up to Memorial Hall. When the Navy owns the Commander-in-Chief's Trophy, it is displayed in the Rotunda.

One of the many halls within Bancroft Hall, Smoke Hall is below Memorial Hall. It is closed to the public and used for various activities by the Brigade of Midshipmen. Along with Memorial Hall and the Rotunda, Smoke Hall was restored in 1994 to its original Beaux-Arts grandeur, which included cleaning the marble and bringing all the light fixtures and electrical systems up to the current code.

The second hospital (labeled Sick Quarters on this photograph) was completed in 1853 in the vicinity of the present officer's club. It was a brick three-story building with wards, a small dispensary, quarters for the medical staff, and a kitchen. It was abandoned with the rest of the academy grounds during the Civil War between 1861 and 1865. It resumed as a hospital in 1865 and as a dispensary after the third hospital was built. The building was in use from 1853 to 1907.

Visitors who enter Gate 3 see the historic chapel to the right and the Mahan, Sampson, and Maury academic buildings at front and left. This entrance has been featured in numerous films, including *Patriot Games*, starring Harrison Ford. This is the scene where Ford's character, Jack Ryan, is attacked while walking to his car on Maryland Avenue. The gate and the gatehouse are some of the oldest structures on the academy grounds.

An empty dining hall is ready and waiting for the next midshipmen to sit, eat, and socialize for a meal sometime in 1881. Today's dining facility, King Hall, is much larger, serving a 4,400-member brigade three times a day. The state-of-the-art dining facility is named after Fleet Adm. Ernest King.

A team of women press freshly washed bed linens in the 1890s. Today, the Naval Academy Laundry and Dry-Cleaning Facility provides a full-service program to the Brigade of Midshipmen and Academy Service Organizations that includes pick-up, processing, and delivery of all laundry. Midshipmen can also access shoe repair and tailors to ensure they look their best.

MARINE BARRACKS. - ANNAPOLIS, MD.

Halligan Hall, constructed in 1903, serves as the public works department for the academy. Before its current role, it served as the US Marine barracks. Marines provided security for the academy from 1851 to 2006. Prior to 2001, they offered a variety of services to the academy, including a 24-hour watch over the tomb of John Paul Jones. The building is now named after Adm. John Halligan (USNA, 1898), a veteran of the Spanish-American War and World War I. He received the Distinguished Service Medal for his service in the former.

Taken in 1873, this photograph shows the entrance to the Superintendent's Residence. At the time, the superintendent of the academy was Commodore John L. Worden. His family is pictured on the steps. Originally used as the Commandant's Headquarters at Fort Severn, the home was demolished in 1901.

One of the oldest buildings at the academy, Buchanan House has been home to the superintendent since 1906. It also has hosted numerous receptions and events, and holds an extensive collection of antiques and Navy memorabilia. In April 2023, Buchanan House was renamed Farragut House in honor of Adm. David Farragut, hero of the Civil War and the first Hispanic officer to hold the rank of admiral.

Chauvenet Hall houses the departments of mathematics, oceanography, and physics, and is named after William Chauvenet, an early professor of mathematics, astronomy, navigation, and surveying at the academy. Michelson Hall is home to the departments of chemistry and economics. In the late 1870s, a Navy lieutenant and instructor in the academy's Physics Department, Albert Michelson, performed his now-famous experiments to measure the velocity of light. These experiments were fundamental to the eventual development of Einstein's theory of relativity. In 1907, Michelson, a graduate of the Naval Academy class of 1873, was the first American to be awarded the Nobel Prize.

Erected in 1905, Isherwood Hall was the home of the Department of Marine Engineering for almost its entire existence. The building was the site of the education of America's future naval officers in the changing technology of steam propulsion. Along with several other structures, it was demolished in the early 1980s to make room for Alumni Hall.

Yard Patrol Craft, or YPs, are used to teach familiarization with watercraft, damage control, and Basic to Advanced Seamanship and Navigation. They provide realistic, at-sea training in navigation and seamanship for midshipmen. They can cruise for 1,800 nautical miles at 12 knots for five days without refueling. This class is 108 feet long and has a beam (width) of 24 feet. The crew complement includes 2 officers, 2 enlisted personnel, and up to 24 midshipmen. This is Yard Patrol Craft 690.

Melville Hall was constructed in 1937, part of the Isherwood complex of engineering buildings. It was named after Rear Adm. George Melville, an early Arctic explorer and proponent of steam engineering. He also established a steam engineering experiment facility in Annapolis. Replaced by Alumni Hall in the early 1980s, Melville is now memorialized as one of the entrances to Alumni Hall.

The Naval Academy once had its own dairy farm to provide milk to dining halls. The farm was purchased in 1913 after numerous midshipmen fell ill after drinking tainted milk. It was in operation until 1988. Pigs were also raised on the farm, and were used to consume food waste from the academy.

Hopper Hall is named for Rear Adm. Grace Hopper, an accomplished mathematician who joined the US Navy Reserve during World War II. She helped develop the UNIVAC computer and assisted in converting mathematical concepts into computer code. This would later be the basis for COBOL. Hopper served in the Navy Reserve for 43 years, retiring in 1986. Hopper Hall is home to midshipmen in cyberoperations, computer engineering, computer science, electrical engineering, information technology, and robotics and control engineering majors, as well as to laboratories for naval architecture and ocean engineering and physics majors.

This modern photograph shows the academy from above in 2015. The only building not present in the photograph is Hopper Hall.

Two

MEMORIALS AND MONUMENTS

The Jeannette Monument was erected for the men who perished in the US Arctic Expedition in October 1881. The 33-man crew of the USS *Jeannette* was trapped in ice and languished in the cold for two years, with two thirds of them dying. The design of the monument is based on a cairn that a recovery crew built to mark the remains of the explorers in the Arctic. The plaque on the monument reads: "Commemorative of the heroic officers and men of the United States Navy who perished in the Jeannette Arctic Exploring Expedition. 1881." The ice on the cross is a reminder of the frigid environment in which they were lost. This is the largest monument at the Naval Academy Cemetery.

This bell is an exact replica of the 15th-century Japanese temple bell that Commodore Matthew Perry brought back from Japan. It was one of the many gifts received as part of an exchange between the United States and Japan during his ambassadorial visit. In 1987, the original bell was returned to Japan. The inscription reads, "Replica of the Temple Bell presented in 1854 to Commodore M.C. Perry, USN, by the Regent of the Lew Chew Islands (Okinawa)."

12

This "Don't Give Up the Ship" replica flag can be viewed at the top of the stairs leading to Memorial Hall in Bancroft Hall. The famous words were first spoken by James Lawrence, captain of USS *Chesapeake*, during the War of 1812 after he was mortally wounded. Commodore Oliver Hazard Perry, impressed with Lawrence's heroism, had the quote stitched onto his battle ensign and subsequently flown over his ship, USS *Lawrence*. The original flag is preserved at the Naval Academy Museum.

A group of plebes (fourth-class midshipmen) salute the Don't Give up the Ship flag in Bancroft Hall. The inscription below the flag reads, "Dedicated to the honor of those alumni who have been killed in action defending the ideals of their country. With immortal value and the price of their lives, these proved their love of their country and their loyalty to the high traditions of their alma mater by inscribing with their own blood the narrative of their deeds above, on, and beneath the seven seas they have set the course they silently stand watch wherever Navy ships ply the waters of the globe."

Lost in Havana Harbor in February 1898, the explosion-bent foremast of USS Maine is on display on the academy grounds. Two hundred and sixty naval personnel died during the explosion. Although reports varied at the time about the cause of the explosion (including a Spanish attack), it is now widely accepted that powder charges destined for the ship's large guns detonated. The plaque on the memorial reads "Foremast of The USS Maine. Ship blew up, Havana 15, Feb, 1898. Mast recovered 6, Oct, 1910. Erected here 5, May, 1913." The mainmast of the Maine is on permanent display about 40 miles away at Arlington National Cemetery, so sailors often call the two masts the "longest ship in the Navy."

This monument honors Naval Academy graduates killed or missing in action in the Vietnam Conflict. It was dedicated on May 17, 1975. The ceremony was attended by Adm. Arleigh Burke, US Navy (Ret.), and hosted by Vice Adm. William P. Mack, superintendent of the academy. Together, they unveiled the six-by-four-foot marker of polished spartan pink granite. On a bronze plaque on the monument are 118 names and the inscription: "In grateful remembrance of Naval Academy graduates killed or missing in action in the Vietnam Conflict." These names are also on display in Memorial Hall, along with the names of all graduates who died in service to their country.

Over 50 submarines were lost during service in World War II. While serving aboard submarines during the war, 3,505 officers and enlisted men lost their lives. Many of the officers lost were Naval Academy graduates. As the monument states at the top, these men are "still on patrol." The quote from Fleet Admiral Nimitz states, "We shall never forget that it was our submarines that held the lines against the enemy while our fleets replaced losses and repaired wounds." The memorial also includes a quote from the commander of submarine forces during World War II, Vice Adm. Charles Lockwood, as well as the names of the 52 submarines on eternal patrol.

The Japanese Pagoda, also known as the Saito Monument, is a 13-tier memorial to Japanese ambassador to the United States Hiroshi Saitō. Saitō was a long-term friend of Pres. Franklin Roosevelt, having served as attaché to Washington when Roosevelt was secretary of the Navy. He spent much of his time in Washington promoting good relations between Japan and the United States. This was especially difficult after Japan sank the USS *Panay* in the Yangtze River in China in 1937. Saitō died of tuberculosis while serving as ambassador in 1939 and his remains were returned to Japan onboard the USS *Astoria* by order of President Roosevelt. Unfortunately, the same ship that humbly delivered his remains to his grateful family was sunk by Japanese forces in 1942. The pagoda was presented to the Naval Academy by Saitō's wife and children in 1940 "in grateful appreciation of American sympathy and courtesy."

The 25-foot tall Triton Light, a working navigation light, was erected in 1959 utilizing donations from the class of 1945. A globe within the monument contains water collected by USS *Triton* during the first submerged circumnavigation of the world in 1960. It is dedicated "to the safe return of all those who go down to the sea in ships." According to a class of 1945 representative, the light's sequence—four-five, four-five—represents the class of 1945. The class's crest can also be seen on the light's base.

This monument is across the street from Mahan Hall. It is the figurehead of the HMS *Macedonian*, captured by Stephen Decatur in command of the frigate USS *United States* in the first year of the War of 1812. It was brought to the academy in 1875. The *United States* was one of the original six frigates authorized by Congress in 1794. The monument has been restored twice, first by the class of 1925 and again by the class of 1967.

Dedicated in 1848 to the memory of four fallen midshipmen, the Mexican War Monument is the longest-standing monument on Naval Academy grounds. None of these midshipmen actually set foot on the then-new Annapolis campus, but their bravery and sacrifice were integral to saving the fledgling Naval Academy. It is located at the intersection of the Stribling and Chapel Walks. The surrounding horizontal cannons are Spanish 12-pounder smooth-bore bronze guns captured in 1847 by the US Navy from Mexicans in California. The midshipmen were H.A. Clemson and J.R. Hynson lost with USS *Somers* off Vera Cruz in 1846; J.W. Pillsbury, drowned off Vera Cruz in 1846; and T.B. Shubrick, killed near Vera Cruz in 1847.

This large stained-glass window shows Jesus Christ with his hands raised. The inscription reads, "In memory of those who Perished in the Samoan hurricane, March 16, 1889." The window was restored by Edward J. Berwind (USNA, 1869). It was originally located in the old chapel. When the old chapel was razed, the window was stored until 1930. It is now located in Bancroft Hall.

Fleet Adm. Chester W. Nimitz (USNA, 1905) was the commander in chief of the US Pacific Fleet during World War II. He was also instrumental in the shift from diesel to nuclear power for the nation's submarine forces. His last assignment was as chief of naval operations from 1945 to 1947. Nimitz died in 1966, and is buried at the Golden Gate National Cemetery in San Bruno, California, along with three other notable Naval Academy graduates: Adm. Raymond A. Spruance, Adm. Richmond K. Turner, and Adm. Charles A. Lockwood, along with their spouses. This bust is displayed at the library named for him at the academy.

Great Mortar Gun, U. S. Naval Academy.

This stereo view shows a great mortar gun on display at the academy. The large-caliber mortar sits upon a platform with ammunition neatly stacked behind. Two officers or cadets are seated on the gun. The photograph likely had some kind of advertisement on the rear, which was a common practice. The gun pictured is a US Army 13-inch rail-mounted gun from the Civil War that was nicknamed the "Dictator." Soldiers would stuff whatever they could into the barrel, including wood, and launch it at the enemy.

The Polaris A1 missile at center was the first nuclear-armed solid-fuel ballistic missile intended for launch from a submarine. They were in service from 1961 to 1980. The type-93 Japanese torpedo at left was the largest ship-launched torpedo in Japan's arsenal in World War II. Over 29 feet long and 24 inches in diameter, it carried over 1,000 pounds of explosives. The torpedo was presented to the academy by Capt. R.M. Fortson. The howitzer at right is a carriage-mounted field gun from the Civil War designed by Rear Adm. John A. Dahlgren, whose name is often associated with it.

The guns pictured here were once used for ceremonial salutes and signals. This photograph is from 1890. None of the buildings in the background remain.

USS *Princeton* was a Navy warship launched in 1843. She had two large guns mounted, named "Peacemaker" and "Oregon." In 1844, Peacemaker exploded during a demonstration, killing six men including Secretary of State Abel Upshur and Secretary of the Navy Thomas Walker Gilmer and injuring 20 others. Pres. John Tyler was aboard but was not injured. More government officials were killed on this day than any other in history. Oregon is pictured here.

This Spanish 12-pounder bronze smooth-bore gun, named "St. Damien," was captured by the US Navy from Mexico in California in 1847 during the Mexican-American War. It is located on the southeast corner of the Mexican War Monument.

This is a Hotchkiss one-pound rapid-fire gun captured from Spain in 1898 during the Spanish-American War. It is on the west side of the parking area in front of Dahlgren Hall. A corner of Ward Hall is seen to the left of the gun. This gun was capable of firing 68 rounds per minute with an accuracy of over one mile. This ship-mounted example was primarily used for torpedo boat defense. Benjamin Hotchkiss was an American military engineer who moved to France in the late 1860s and established a respected arms and ammunition company.

It could easily be argued that the US Naval Academy Cemetery and Columbarium is the largest memorial on campus. Located on a peninsula overlooking the Severn River and College Creek, the cemetery is the final resting place for hundreds of the nation's veterans, many of whom gave their lives in service to their country. It is a record of children mourning lost parents, parents mourning lost children, a nation mourning lost heroes, and a school mourning lost classmates. It is also a record of accomplishments: Medal of Honor recipients, a chief of naval operations, superintendents of the academy, midshipmen, and former employees are among those buried there. Veterans of every major American war, including those lost to accidents in times of peace, are also buried here.

TRIPOLI MONUMENT.

The oldest military monument in the United States, the Tripoli Monument honors naval heroes of the First Barbary War (1801–1805). The monument was created in Italy and brought to the United States in 1806 onboard the USS *Constitution*. It was originally on display at the Washington Navy Yard and in front of the US Capitol. It has been on display in Annapolis since 1860. The inscription on the monument is quite long, but a smaller brass plaque summarizes it well: "The oldest military monument in the United States honors heroes of the War against the Barbary Coast Pirates, the new republic's first war. In 1804, President Jefferson ordered the nation's tiny naval force to the Mediterranean to protect the expanding trade of the new United States against the pirates, who demanded ransom for safe passage of merchant ships. 'Millions for defense, but not one cent for tribute' became the rallying cry for this war. Jefferson's action established the doctrine of extension of power overseas and created a permanent United States Navy."

This late-19th-century photograph shows the Tripoli Monument as it looked before any of the Flagg buildings were constructed. None of the other structures in this photograph remain today.

This statue depicts the academy mascot, Bill the Goat. He has been on display in some form since 1957. Visitors can see Bill inside Gate 1 at the intersection of King George Street and Cooper Road. In the past, goats were often taken aboard Navy ships because they could consume much of the garbage the crew created. Legend has it that one crew took a liking to their goat, and when it died, they had it memorialized by a taxidermist. Navy was playing football that weekend, and the two midshipmen assigned the task attended the game. At halftime, they used the goat skin as a makeshift blanket and hopped around the field. Bill the Goat has been the academy mascot since 1890; the current goat is Bill XXXVII.

This photograph was taken by Mrs. C.R. Miller on January 26, 1913, the day John Paul Jones was laid to rest in his crypt below the chapel. Since 1906, his coffin had previously been in the Academy Chapel inside Bancroft Hall. (Courtesy of Navy History and Heritage Command).

John Paul Jones's crypt was designed by Beaux-Arts architect Whitney Warren, and the 21-ton sarcophagus and surrounding columns of black and white Royal Pyrenees marble were the work of sculptor Sylvain Salieres. The sarcophagus is supported by bronze dolphins and is embellished with cast garlands of bronze sea plants. Inscribed in brass letters around the base are the names of the ships commanded by Jones during the American Revolution: *Providence, Alfred, Ranger, Bonhomme Richard, Serapis, Alliance,* and *Ariel.* American flags and union jacks are placed between the marble columns. Set in brass in the marble floor at the head of the sarcophagus is the inscription: "John Paul Jones, 1747–1792 / U.S. Navy 1775–1783 / He Gave Our Navy Its Earliest Traditions / Of Heroism And Victory / Erected by the Congress, A.D. 1912." Important objects related to Jones's life and naval career are exhibited in niches around the periphery. Jones died in Paris at the age of 45. He was initially interred in the St. Louis Cemetery, home to French royalty. Over 100 years later and after much searching, he was brought home.

606

Incorrectly known by many as "Tecumseh," Tamanend was the figurehead from the USS *Delaware*. *Delaware* was sunk by the Union early in the Civil War to prevent her capture by the Confederacy. The figurehead was originally made of wood. However, it was cast and preserved in bronze in 1891. In 1930, it was mounted on a pedestal of Vermont marble and placed in its current location, where it watches over the Brigade of Midshipmen in front of the main entrance to Bancroft Hall. The monument is frequently painted by the brigade to rally the midshipmen for an upcoming sports game.

The Herndon Monument is named for Comdr. William Lewis Herndon, 1813–1857, who possessed the qualities of discipline, teamwork, and courage. In command of the SS *Central America* and homebound with gold-seekers from California, the ship encountered a three-day hurricane off the coast of North Carolina. Herndon went down with his ship after a gallant effort to save it, its sailors, and passengers. This monument was erected on the Yard in his honor shortly after his death. Most visitors know the monument for the Herndon Climb, which takes place each spring. Plebes are required to remove their shoes prior to starting the climb. Over the years, thousands of these athletic shoes have been donated by the plebe classes to various charities through the Midshipman Action Group. Demonstrating the teamwork and perseverance they learned during their first year at the academy, the plebes build a human pyramid to remove the "dixie cup" hat at the top of the vegetable shortening–covered monument and replace it with an upperclassman's hat. After successfully completing the Herndon Climb, the freshmen are no longer called plebes but "fourth class midshipmen." It is a must-see event in Annapolis toward the end of May. The brush surrounding the monument in this photograph has been cleared.

Situated near the USS *Maine* memorial, this bell was carried by the USS *Paddle* throughout World War II. The *Paddle* was named for a large fish that is common in the Mississippi River. The monument memorializes the 52 American submarines and the 3,621 sailors who were lost at sea. It also pays tribute to submarines *Thresher* and *Scorpion*, both lost at sea in the 1960s. The bottom of the memorial reads: "May the list end here. Sailor rest your oar."

In October 1864, Union commander William B. Cushing (USNA, 1861), 1842–1874, led a crew that attacked and sank the Confederate ironclad CSS *Albemarle*. His monument is topped by an elaborate relief that depicts drapery, a service dress hat, and a sword.

This mural depicts the US brig *Niagara*, flagship of Master Commandant Oliver Hazard Perry, raking the British warships *Queen Charlotte* and *Detroit*, which are afoul of each other after colliding. *Niagara* is flying Perry's Don't Give Up the Ship battle flag at her mainmast peak. This mural, presented to the US Naval Academy by Adm Thomas C. Hart and his wife, Caroline, is on display in the academy's Memorial Hall. It was created by Charles Robert Patterson and Howard B. French in 1959. (Courtesy of Navy History and Heritage Command.)

This British royal standard flew over York (Toronto), Canada, and was captured by US forces during the War of 1812. Congressional and presidential directives for more than 150 years have required the US Naval Academy to preserve and exhibit captured flags. This one was previously in an exhibit case in Mahan Hall, where only a portion of the flag was viewable. Along with several War of 1812 ship flags captured by the US Navy, the standard was removed after a century for curation.

This columbarium is adjacent to the cemetery on College Creek. It was built in 1987 utilizing funds from the Naval Academy Alumni Association and the George and Mary Olmstead Foundation, in memory of Jerauld Olmstead (USNA, 1922). The memorial is 160 feet long and made primarily of marble. It is a final resting place option for those who have been cremated.

Vice Adm. William M. Beakley (center), commander of the US Seventh Fleet, accepts on behalf of the academy a Japanese stone lantern from Yokohama's mayor Ryozo Hironuma (left) in a ceremony aboard the admiral's flagship, USS *Saint Paul* (CA-73), in 1958. The seven-foot high, 4,000-pound lantern is symbolic of the friendship between Japan and the United States, especially the citizens of Yokohama and Navy and Marine Corps personnel who have served in the Far East. It was installed on the grounds of the Navy–Marine Corps Memorial Stadium in Annapolis.

Three

THE MIDSHIPMEN

THE NAVAL ACADEMY BALL AT ANNAPOLIS, MARYLAND, JANUARY 8, 1869.—SKETCHED BY THEO. R. DAVIS.—[SEE PAGE 71.]

"Waltz me around again, Admiral," reads the description on this photograph, discovered in the Naval Academy library archives. Balls such as the one depicted, in January 1869, would have been the hottest ticket in Annapolis. The young ladies would wear colorful dresses and would be led around the parquet dance floor by their midshipmen partners.

Two midshipmen enjoy a game of chess in 1873. The young man to the left is Albert Michelson (he graduated the year of this photograph), the noted mathematician who calculated the speed of light when he was posted to the academy as an instructor in 1879. It would be fascinating to discover who won the game!

These two midshipmen enjoy some quiet time in their dorm room in 1899 at the New Quarters, the predecessor to Bancroft Hall. Each student has his own sink, mirror, and toiletry area. The room is also decorated with some personal items, including a couple of pictures of possible sweethearts. At least one of the midshipmen is smoking a cigar, which is most definitely not permitted today.

This 1878 art classroom features quite a few sculptures, large and small, for students to practice their artistic skills. Although not clear in the photograph, the pages hanging against the walls are likely studies done by the midshipmen. The professor's desk is at right on the platform.

This photograph was taken for the 1923 *Lucky Bag*, the Naval Academy yearbook. This class was in radio engineering. At the time, radio transmission and broadcast were in their infancy. The first transatlantic radio transmission was performed by Guglielmo Marconi in 1901. This is likely all Marconi-branded equipment. Eight midshipmen are present with their professor (center).

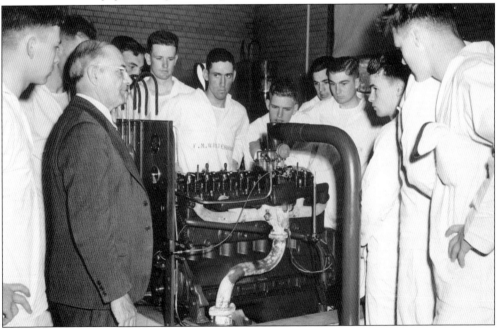

Eleven midshipmen (all plebes) study a small diesel engine with their professor. Once these students got out to sea, they would be expected to understand the design and maintenance of the engines that powered the Navy's ships and boats. These young men would have graduated from the academy in 1949.

First-class midshipmen climb aboard the Electronics Field Laboratory barge for some hands-on learning in 1949. Instruction in the laboratory included radar, sonar, and loran (long-range navigation). A radar antenna is visible on the upper deck of the barge. The class instructor, Lt. Comdr. Rue O'Neill, is at the head of the gangway greetings his students. Numbered YF-89, the classroom barge would have been acquired well before World War II.

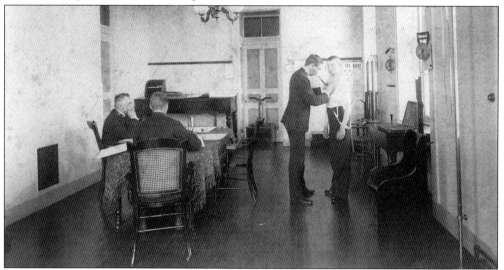

This photograph, taken on one of the wards on the upper floors of the Sick Quarters Building in 1892, features a midshipman undergoing a physical examination. At far left is the academy's chief medical inspector and senior medical officer, Thomas Cameron Walton. Conducting the exam is the academy's surgeon, William Richards DuBose. During the 19th century, hopeful naval cadet candidates presented themselves for academic and physical examinations twice annually, once in May and again in September. According to the annual register for 1892, the following were medical reasons for rejection: "feeble constitution; retarded development; impaired general health; cachexia, diathesis, or predisposition to disease; and any disease, deformity, or result of injury that would impair efficiency." Candidates also had to meet height and weight standards, much like they do today.

Members of the class of 1892 pose for a photograph in their dress uniforms. Notable members of the class include Rear Adm. John Blakely (awarded the Navy Cross for his service in World War I), Rear Adm. George Day (also awarded the Navy Cross for service in World War I), Capt. Edward Kellogg (a former naval governor of American Samoa), Adm. Luke McNamee (former president of the Naval War College), and Maj. Gen. John Russell (former commandant of the Marine Corps).

Members of the class of 1861 pose for a photograph. Midshipman George M. Bache is third from left. He later served as the commanding officer of several Union vessels during the Civil War. To the right of Bache is William F. Stewart, later lost at sea while serving as executive officer onboard USS *Oneida*. Midshipman Richard F. Armstrong (second from right) resigned his US Navy commission in 1861 and served in the Confederate navy.

Midshipmen enjoy a meal in 1887. The class of 1887 had 44 graduates. Multiply that by four, and the total Brigade of Midshipmen was about 150. Today, midshipmen eat in King Hall, and the facility and its outstanding staff feed over 4,000 men and women three times a day!

The Brigade of Midshipmen assembles for general muster in 1887. Men in leadership positions stand in front of and behind their respective companies. This is a tradition that continues today. The Tamanend Monument is visible in the background.

The Naval Academy boxing team is pictured here in the late 1920s. Boxing has had a place at the academy since 1865. Up until the early 20th century, it was considered a leisure activity. Now, the academy has boxing clubs and hosts the annual Brigade Boxing Tournament, featuring male and female athletes separated by weight class. The best boxers can compete at the National Collegiate Boxing Championships each spring.

Given the subject matter on the chalkboard, this is a mathematics class. Each midshipman has been given his section of the board by the professor with a different problem to solve. The other students and the professor watch. Although the location is not labeled, the photograph is from the late 19th century, so it does not exist today.

A group of midshipmen, including future admiral James O. Richardson, sit on a second-class midshipmen bench near the Tripoli Monument in 1902. As the commander-in-chief of the US fleet in 1940, Admiral Richardson warned leadership in Washington that it would be best to maintain a strong defense at Pearl Harbor because it and Guam were not prepared for any kind of hostility with Japan. As Admiral Richardson was a longtime authority in Japanese warfare, President Roosevelt should have listened to him. He was fired instead. Pearl Harbor was attacked just 10 months later.

A soon-to-be commissioned US Navy officer receives his diploma from Pres. Theodore Roosevelt in 1902. It is a tradition that the president of the United States visits one of the service academies for graduation ceremonies each year. Therefore, he or she visits the Naval Academy every four years. In the off years, the academy receives the vice president, secretary of the Navy, and chief of naval operations or chairman of the Joint Chiefs of Staff.

A group of plebes learn how to safely operate the M-1 rifle in 1950. The instructors are Marines attached to the Naval Academy. The M1 rifles seen in the photograph were in service from 1936 to 1958. All Marines, whether officers or enlisted, learn to use and maintain small arms. Newly commissioned US Marine Corps officers leave the Naval Academy with the weapons they have trained on.

This panoramic image includes the Brigade of Midshipmen with Bancroft Hall in the background. It was taken in December 1920. The class of 1920 graduated the year prior to this photograph (1919) because they were a wartime accelerated class. Earlier in 1920, the Navy crew team won a gold medal at the Olympic games in Belgium.

Members of the class of 1905 enjoy a pipe and some good time together in 1904. This was the first year midshipmen were allowed to have and use a pipe. Most of the midshipmen in the photograph have been identified. They are, in unknown order, John Sumpter, Isaac Dortch, John Newton, William Spears, Gordon Haines, John Mandeville, Sylvester Lawton, Herbert Leary, Henry Rawle, Clarence Grace, William Eberle, Lloyd Townsend, Lee Border, William Culbertson, and Malcolm Campbell.

This 1874 photograph shows members of the class of 1878. They had all begun their studies that year. Most of the students have been identified. By number, they are 1. C. Cunningham, 3. J.H. Hetherington, 4. F. Swift, 5. P.B. Bibb, 6. J.A. Dougherty, 7. H.L. Sturdevant, 9. James B. Cahoon, 11. G.H. Stafford, 13. P.O. Conger, 15. John Gibson, 16. A.G. Rodgers, 17. G.R. Clark, 18. J.H.L. Holcombe, 20. P.L. Drayton, 21. C.A. Mayer, 22. H.S. Knapp, 23. J.J. Knapp, 24. John Hood, 25. J.G. Quimby, 26. E. Lloyd Jr., 27. W.L. Rodgers, 28. W.J. Maxwell, 29. S. Biddle, and 30. F.H. Duer.

Midshipmen participate in a gunnery exercise onboard a training vessel near Annapolis in 1887. The ship is unidentified, but she is likely a frigate that had exceeded her life expectancy and was stationed at the academy as a training ship. She might be the USS *Wyoming*.

Two midshipmen take a moment to make some alterations to their jackets in 1896. The young man at right might be closing a hole in his jacket, while the young man at left looks to be struggling with threading the needle.

A group of four midshipmen in their dress uniforms work together to scale the brick wall that surrounds the academy grounds. Considering how long it took to take a photograph in 1893, this one is likely staged. However, it is good to know that college antics were alive and well over a hundred years ago.

What did midshipmen do in their spare time in the 1890s? They played the guitar, banjo, and flute, and others read the paper. One midshipman is enjoying a cigarette, which was a violation of rules at the time.

A group of spectators including midshipmen and active-duty personnel watch as the bronze doors to the US Naval Academy Chapel are unveiled in 1913. The doors are 22 feet tall and 8 feet wide, so they tower over midshipmen, newlyweds, and tourists who pass through them. One door depicts the idea of science contemplating war, and the other depicts a mother showing her son how to fight. The doors went through a major restoration in 2018 funded by the class of 1968.

A four-man crew team rows in sync on the Severn River in 1932. They are all plebes, and they are likely learning the ropes from more senior rowers. Navy crew has a long and storied history, including trips to the Olympic games.

Fourteen members of the Naval Academy football team are pictured in 1895. The team went 5-2 that year. Games at that time were played on the grounds of the academy at Worden Field. Today, the team plays at the Navy–Marine Corps Memorial Stadium in Annapolis.

Three midshipmen swab the deck of USS *Indiana* (BB-1) during their 1902 summer cruise. From left to right are Chester W. Nimitz, G. Stewart, and Royal Ingersoll. The photograph comes courtesy of the private collection of Fleet Adm. Chester W. Nimitz.

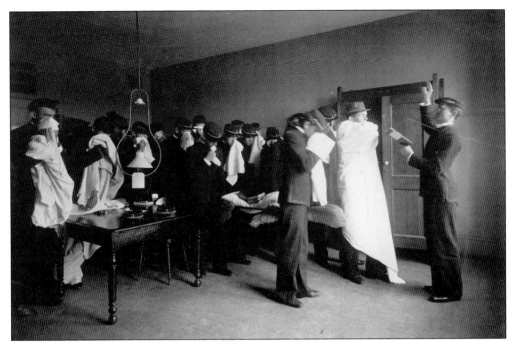

Future leaders of the Navy celebrate the end of classes. In this case, it is math and physics. At the time of this photograph, the celebration called "Burial of Math and Skinny" was a big deal, with the master of ceremonies getting a tag line in the *Lucky Bag* yearbook. The practice is now prohibited.

A group of midshipmen indoctrinate new members of the company, likely all plebes. Two midshipmen are standing on their heads (with pillows), one is under the table, one is standing at attention, and another is in the wardrobe. Hazing activities like this existed well into the 20th century but were essentially outlawed in 1950, when the practice became a punishable offense under the Uniform Code of Military Justice.

A group of midshipmen listen and sing while another plays the piano in Smoke Hall. At the time of the photograph in 1911, Smoke Hall, which is inside Bancroft Hall, would have been just five years old. To this day, it remains a place for midshipmen to gather.

In this undated photograph, midshipmen walk from Bancroft Hall to their classes along Stribling Walk. They are most likely headed to the Sampson/Maury academic buildings for liberal arts instruction. The Tamanend Monument (also known as Tecumseh and Delaware) is in the background, facing Bancroft Hall.

A group of hungry midshipmen look at the upcoming menu posted to the mess hall door in 1925. In reality, these midshipmen look to be taking down the weekly menu so they can bring the good news back to their companies.

Have you wondered what a formal drill (parade) at the academy would be like a hundred years ago? For the most part, they looked quite the same as they do today. Midshipmen marched around a designated parade field while visitors and parents watched with pride and awe. In this 1890 photograph, the midshipmen finish a parade with a gun salute. No parents were harmed in the production of this image.

A midshipman winds a clock to ensure it keeps accurate time. The location of the clock is unknown, but it is likely in his room. The photograph was taken for the 1926 *Lucky Bag* by White Studios.

In the past, all midshipmen were required to learn about aviation and receive flight training. In this 1925 photograph, Assistant Secretary of the Navy Theodore Douglas Robinson prepares to take a flight with Midshipman Larson, who has already received his training. Also in the photograph is Adm. Louis B. Nutton, superintendent of the academy.

A group of midshipmen (plebes) sit on a pier in 1925 and receive instruction from the military instructor on the seaplane they are going to learn to fly. The cemetery and original Naval Academy Bridge are in the background.

If asked today, midshipmen might say that their counterparts 100 years ago were limited in their extracurricular activities. This photograph, taken in Smoke Hall, proves otherwise. Here, four midshipmen play what appears to be two-against-two billiards in the 1920s.

In the past, all personnel in the military headed to the pay office every two weeks and were paid in cash. Later, they received a US government check. Today, every person who works for the federal government is required to maintain the ability to receive their pay via direct deposit.

The annual midshipman summer cruise of 1890 was held onboard the USS *Constellation*, the second naval vessel to bear the name. She was in service from 1854 to 1933 and is now a museum ship in Baltimore, Maryland. During this period, midshipmen engaged in sailing and military activities separated from vessels engaged in real-world activities. In 1912, the Navy started sending midshipmen to ships in active service throughout the fleet.

Filmed on location at the academy in 1925, the silent film *The Midshipmen* starred Roman Navarro, Harriett Hammond, and a 19-year-old Joan Crawford driving a police car. The film revolves around a few men, a beautiful woman, a dance, and a yacht. In the end, the young midshipman retains his honor and marries the girl.

This undated photograph shows the class of 1956, including Charlie Wilson. Wilson served in the Navy for four years, but is most known as the Texas congressman who supported Operation Cyclone, the covert CIA operation that supported the Afghan mujahideen from 1979 to 1992.

This is the dance from the film *The Midshipmen*. While the dance is taking place, an attempt is made by a lady named Rita to discredit Midshipman Ted Lawrence while he is on watch at the academy guardhouse. Unfortunately, he is not there. Instead, Midshipman James Randall watches his friend with Rita and chooses to resign instead of reporting the incident involving his best friend. Once he finds out the true nature of the incident, he revokes his resignation and marries the woman of his dreams, Patricia.

Midshipmen listen to their instructor on Induction Day (I-Day) 1976 as they learn important information they will need moving forward. This was the first year that women were allowed to attend the academy. Four years later, 55 women graduated from the academy.

Skippers of the five academy 44-foot Luders yawls participating in the tall ship race from Bermuda to New York receive their Operation Sail '76 pennants from Annapolis committeeman George Wilson (left) at the Robert Crown Center. Skippers (and their yawls) are, from left to right, Ensigns Jim Hann, *Active*; Don Thieme, *Restless*; and Dale Dykuizen, *Flirt*; Midshipman First Class Dan Gearing, *Dandy*; and Midshipman First Class Harold Gretzky, *Fearless*. The five yawls, with their midshipmen crews, raced in company with sail training ships from all over the world. The yawls joined other Operation Sail '76 participants in New York City on July Fourth, representing the Naval Academy in a naval review before President Ford as part of the country's bicentennial celebration.

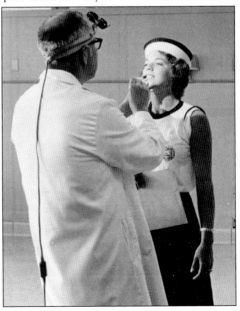

As part of their first summer at the academy, midshipmen are put through a battery of medical tests, including oral health. Here, a dentist determines whether this midshipman requires a follow-up visit in 1976. The student has been identified as Chrystal A. Lewis from Alexandria, Virginia. Lewis later became an A-4E Skyhawk pilot in the Navy. She was among the first group of women to attend the academy.

All of the service academies welcome students from around the world to receive a world-class education. In some cases, students spend all four years at the academy because their respective countries do not have military academies. In this photograph, two Iranian midshipmen (plebes) are welcomed to the academy by the superintendent, Adm. Kinnaird McKee, in 1976.

Two midshipmen receive training from their military instructor on some new technology making its way to the fleet. Based on what is visible in the picture, it looks to be an audio mixer for communications.

This plaque was presented by the Brigade of Midshipmen to the US Military Academy at West Point in honor of its 150th anniversary in 1952. It reads "Presented to the Corps of Cadets by the Brigade of Midshipmen, United States Naval Academy, in commemoration of the 150th anniversary of the founding of the United States Military Academy."

Learning the ropes had quite a different meaning in the late 19th and early 20th century in the Navy. Sailors had to understand basic knot tying, as well as all the rigging for sailing ships. In this photograph, an instructor and four midshipmen review a precision scale model of a sailing frigate.

Capt. C.H. Harlow, USN (retired), representing the class of 1879, presents a sword to the midshipman regimental commander, class of 1929, on the 50th anniversary of 1879's graduation. While ceremonies like this have been going on for decades, the Another Link in the Chain program was formally established in 2002. According to the USNA website, the program "forms bonds and relationships between current midshipmen and members of the 50-year class counterpart throughout the four years on the Yard and beyond. The midshipmen are buoyed and encouraged by the physical presence and moral support of the senior alumni, and members of the 50-year class counterpart enjoy working with the current midshipmen in their development of Navy and Marine officers. From Induction Day to Commissioning and beyond, the 50-year counterpart class becomes a part of the Naval Academy experience for the Brigade."

Members of the class of 1987 prepare to take the oath of office at the parade grounds at the academy in 1983. All midshipmen take the following oath on their first day at the academy: "Having been appointed a midshipman in the United States Navy, I solemnly swear (or affirm) that I will support and defend the Constitution of the United States against all enemies, foreign and domestic; that I will bear true faith and allegiance to the same; that I take this obligation freely, without any mental reservation or purpose of evasion; and that I will well and faithfully discharge the duties of the office on which I am about to enter, so help me God."

A class of midshipmen learn all there is to know about ship navigation in 1942. The commander in the photograph helps a midshipman with a navigation problem. A full-size ship's compass with binnacle is visible in the left foreground. Officers in the Navy still use similar tools to determine elements like course, range, and bearing both from and to objects when underway.

Two midshipmen from the class of 1987 practice their submarining skills at the Kings Bay, Georgia, Ohio Class Trident Training Facility. Adm. Charles Larson looks on. The midshipman at left is manning the helm, and the one second from right is manning the stern planes. All Ohio-class submarines have fairwater planes, which enable them to control depth without increasing or decreasing pitch. The midshipman at far right is sitting at the chief of the watch console.

Midshipmen pose on the bow of the US Naval Academy yacht *Astral* after returning from a month-long midshipmen's cruise in the Caribbean in 1982. Capt. Barry A. Gastrock, commanding officer and chief navigator of the *Astral*, is at far left in the top row. The *Astral* was a 98-foot luxury yacht used by the Naval Academy for training.

Plebes at the US Naval Academy compete in the annual Rear Admiral Blakely Cup race on the Severn River in 1983. This award was originally presented to the plebe battalion that won the summer Knockabout Championship Race. In 2000, the award was given to the Fall Intramural Sailing Battalion champions. Rear Adm. Charles Blakely (USNA, 1903) had a distinguished career in the Navy, serving for almost 40 years.

The class of 1890 had 34 graduates. One of the many notable members was Wendy C. Neville, commissioned a second lieutenant in the Marine Corps in 1892. He was promoted to captain in 1898 for his outstanding leadership and valor at Guantanamo Bay during the Spanish-American War, and in 1900, he was commended for gallantry for his role in the China Relief Expedition. In 1914, Neville led the Marines ashore at Veracruz, Mexico, and was awarded the Medal of Honor for conspicuous gallantry. During World War I, he commanded the 5th Marines at Belleau Wood and later rose to command of the 4th Marine Brigade. Promoted to major general in 1923, Neville succeeded John Lejeune as commandant on March 5, 1929. He is buried in Arlington National Cemetery.

Outfitted in his full dress uniform, Midshipman Frederick Byron Hull is pictured here, likely around 1865, when the Naval Academy was in Newport during the Civil War.

Four midshipmen enjoy a day out on the Severn River in 1942. The water looks to be a bit choppy, but they seem to be handling it well. The third midshipman's left hand is on the tiller. The fourth is likely taking the photograph.

The nine-member USNA baseball team poses in 1881. Baseball has been played in the United States since the 1850s, with the National Association of Baseball Players being formed in 1867. At the time, the academy had both student and teacher teams. Pictured are, from left to right, (first row) W.M. Robinson and Z.B. Vance; (second row) M.A. Orlopp, M. Craven, T.H. Matthews, and B.G. Pierce; (third row) M.J. Donnelly, L. Karmany, and J. Lindsey. The bat held by Vance has a much larger grip circumference than modern bats.

Midshipmen march past the Naval Academy Chapel to a full-dress parade to be held on campus at Worden Field. Most of the formal parades are open to the public.

The class of 2022 attempts the Herndon Climb in 2019. This annual May event symbolizes the close of the first year for plebes. Upperclassmen make it as difficult as possible by greasing the 21-foot monument with vegetable shortening. Participants must use teamwork, strategy, communication, and a lot of t-shirts to successfully climb the monument. The goal is to reach the top and exchange the dixie cup cover with a traditional midshipman's cap. Once that is done, they are plebes no more. (Photograph by Mass Communication Specialist Third Class Josiah Pearce.)

A plebe crawls his way through a tunnel formed by midshipmen during the annual Sea Trials. Designed after the US Marine Corps Crucible and Battle Stations program at the US Navy boot camp, this is a capstone event for these young men and women. It also serves as a leadership challenge for the senior midshipmen who supervise each event. (Photograph by Mass Communication Specialist First Class Chad Runge.)

A midshipman places one of 2,977 flags along Stribling Walk in remembrance of the lives that were lost on September 11, 2001. Each flag represents one of the lives lost that day at the World Trade Center, Pentagon, and Somerset County, Pennsylvania.

Four

FACULTY, STAFF, EVENTS, VISITORS, AND ALUMNI

While serving as the secretary of the Navy to Pres. James K. Polk, George Bancroft founded the Naval Academy in Annapolis in 1845. The United States did not have a formal place for training midshipmen at the time. Because Annapolis was relatively isolated and therefore able to protect midshipmen from sickness, Congress appropriated the funds necessary to keep the academy going. Bancroft was also a noted historian and statesman. The midshipmen dormitory, the largest in the United States, is named in his honor.

Capt. Franklin Buchanan served as the first superintendent of the newly established Naval Academy from 1845 to 1847. He was appointed to the post by Secretary of the Navy George Bancroft for his efforts in establishing the school. Unfortunately, his legacy became tarnished when he later served in the Confederate navy, achieving the rank of admiral. He was also the commanding officer of the CSS *Virginia* during the Battle of Hampton Roads. The residence of the superintendent bears his name.

This is a photograph of the Mathematics Department in 1906–1907. Seven of the pictured faculty are military. Today, most of the faculty in all departments are civilian government employees.

The Modern Languages Department for 1915–1916 poses in front of Sampson or Maury Hall.

This is a c. 1920s photograph of the English, History, and Government Department taken in front of Bancroft Hall.

The Electrical Engineering Department poses around 1929–1930 in front of Sampson Hall.

This undated photograph of the Weapons Department was taken in front of Dahlgren Hall, likely in the early part of the 20th century.

TOP ROW—W.J.Strother L.J.Kreinbihl G.W.Henderson R.G.Voge R.N.Smoot S.P.Moseley T.G.Haff W.G.Buch
O.R.Swigart C.E.Tolman SECOND ROW—G.Beneze B.H.Johnson E.E.Sprung J.S.Keating F.A.Edwards
J.S.Smith W.M.Callaghan F.D.McCorkle G.M.Brooke R.M.Zimmerll M.C.Barrett W.E.Farrell
THIRD ROW—J.W.Steele J.R.Hanna E.A.Solomons J.C.Lester A.C.Thorington T.M.Dell G.D.Martin
J.C.Eakens A.C.Behan FRONT ROW—E.J.Kidder T.B.Thompson G.A.Rood W.A.Riedel A.M.PENN
T.W.Johnson C.E.Hoard J.B.W.Waller B.F.Perry
1933—1934

The Mechanical Engineering Department is pictured in front of Isherwood Hall.

The Languages Department for 1933–1934 is seen here. The building is unidentified, but most of the faculty have been identified at the bottom of the photograph.

This photograph of the Electrical Engineering and Physics Departments was taken in front of Sampson Hall in the early 20th century.

Alfred Thayer Mahan graduated second in his class at the Naval Academy in 1859. One of his most notable achievements was writing *The Influence of Sea Power Upon History, 1660–1783*. He wrote the book while assigned as a lecturer in naval history and tactics at the Naval War College. *Sea Power* put him among the greatest minds of the 19th century, and he was certainly one of the greatest naval strategists in history. He retired from the Navy as a captain, but was subsequently promoted to rear admiral, as were all captains who served in the Union Navy.

Rear Adm. Edward Simpson, pictured in the 1860s, entered the Navy as a midshipman in 1840. Later, he joined the first class to be trained and educated at the newly established Naval Academy in Annapolis. He served two tours in Annapolis, one as a gunnery instructor and the other as the head of that department. He was instrumental in moving the academy to Newport during the Civil War.

Fleet Adm. Ernest J. King was a 1901 graduate of the Naval Academy. He saw service in the Spanish-American War onboard the USS *San Francisco* while attending school. After the attack on Pearl Harbor, he was named commander-in-chief of the US fleet, and later served as chief of naval operations. He was promoted to fleet admiral in 1944. Here, he is administering the oath of office to a new group of officers in 1944 or 1945.

This photograph from the 1890s shows Comdr. Colby Mitchell Chester, commandant of cadets (left), and Lt. John M. Hawley, assistant commandant, at their desks working on the tasks for the day with respect to leading the Brigade of Midshipmen.

A young Jimmy Carter graduates and receives his ensign bars from his mother, Lillian Carter, and his wife, Rosalynn Carter, in 1946. Carter served in the Navy until 1953, when he returned to Georgia to run his family peanut business. Later, he would serve in the Georgia state senate and as governor of Georgia. In 1976, he was elected the 39th president of the United States. In 2002, he was awarded the Nobel Peace Prize for his humanitarian work with the Carter Center. He lives in Plains, Georgia, with Rosalynn, his wife of 76 years.

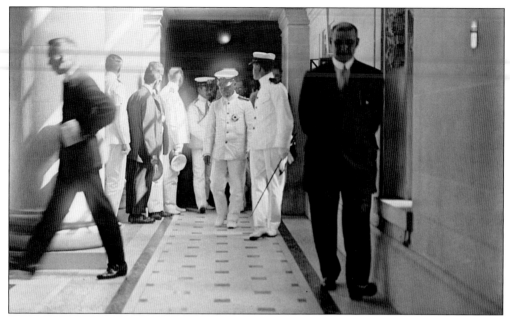

Marshal-Admiral Marquis Tōgō Heihachirō was an admiral of the fleet of the Imperial Japanese Navy. His most notable military achievement was during the Russo-Japanese War of 1904–1905. He was also an honorary knight grand cross of the Victorian Order for Great Britain. He visited the Naval Academy in 1911 while he was admiral of the fleet.

In 1953, Pres. Dwight D. Eisenhower makes a quick inspection on board LSMR-515 after his golf game and before returning to USS *Williamsburg*, which is tied up at the Santee Dock at the US Naval Academy. Vice Adm. C. Turner Joy, superintendent of the Naval Academy, is also pictured between the two lieutenants. An LSMR is a medium-sized landing ship equipped with rockets, mostly operated from the late 1940s to the 1960s.

Fleet Adm. William Leahy, pictured in 1945, was an 1897 graduate of the academy. He was the first of only four individuals to achieve the rank of fleet admiral (followed by Nimitz, King, and Halsey). He had retired from the Navy in 1939, but was recalled to active duty for service in World War II. For most of the war, he served as President Roosevelt's chief of staff, a position that essentially made him second in command for decisions related to the war.

Capt. Robert Pythian was an 1856 graduate of the Naval Academy. After several sea and shore tours, he was assigned as the first superintendent of the New York Nautical School (now SUNY Maritime). He then served as superintendent of the Naval Observatory from 1886 to 1890. Finally, he was superintendent of the US Naval Academy from 1890 to 1894 (pictured).

Maj. Gen. John Russell was an 1892 graduate of the academy. He was appointed commandant of the Marine Corps in 1934. This photograph was likely taken on the day of his turnover to his successor, Gen. Thomas Holcomb. Russell transformed the way that officers were promoted during his tenure, shifting to a selection board format rather than automatic promotion.

From left to right, Adm. William "Bull" Halsey, Secretary of the Navy Frank Knox, and Adm. Ernest J. King are pictured at the Navy Department in Washington after Admiral Halsey received the Distinguished Service Medal (his second) in 1944.

Members of the US Army 3rd Infantry Regiment "The Old Guard" Caisson Platoon parade the black flag–draped casket, escorted by US Forces Honor Guard, of Adm. Thomas H. Moorer during a full military honors burial at Arlington National Cemetery in 2004. Admiral Moorer was a 1933 graduate of the Naval Academy. He served as the chief of naval operations from 1967 to 1970 and chairman of the Joint Chiefs of Staff, a post he held until his retirement in 1974.

John Sidney McCain III was a 1958 graduate of the Naval Academy. He survived the deadly fire onboard the USS *Forrestal* in 1967. Later that year, he was shot down while on a bombing run over Hanoi. He was held as a prisoner of war until 1973. His service in the Navy continued after his release, and he retired as a captain in 1981. For the rest of his life, he continued to serve his country in both the House of Representatives and the Senate. His father and grandfather also graduated from the Naval Academy.

Lt. Comdr. Harold Bartlett prepares to fly his PN-10 nonstop from Hampton Roads to the Canal Zone, a distance of 2,061 miles, in 1926. He received his flight training at Naval Air Station Pensacola, receiving the title Naval Aviator 21. He also earned the Navy Cross for his efforts during World War I.

Wesley Brown was the first African American to graduate from the US Naval Academy, in 1949. He was actually the sixth African American to be admitted to the academy, but the first five dropped out within a year because of relentless hazing. Brown was lucky that he had a few midshipmen who supported and protected him, including first-class midshipman Jimmy Carter. Brown was a civil engineer in the Navy, and rose to the rank of lieutenant commander before retiring in 1969. The Wesley Brown Field House is named in his honor. He died in 2012.

On the morning of December 7, 1941, Capt. Mervyn Bennion was drinking his morning coffee aboard his ship USS *West Virginia* (BB-48) when the first Japanese bombs hit. Over the next few hours, he heroically directed casualty and response efforts, even though he was mortally wounded. Bennion refused to be evacuated from his ship on several occasions. He was awarded the Medal of Honor for his efforts.

Just one year after his graduation in 1944, Lt. Richard M. McCool is presented with the Medal of Honor by Pres. Harry S. Truman at the White House. The medal was awarded for saving the entire crew of a destroyer that was sinking while he was also under attack. His citation reads, in part, "By his staunch leadership, capable direction and indomitable determination throughout the crisis, Lieutenant McCool saved the lives of many who otherwise might have perished and contributed materially to the saving of his ship for further combat service. His valiant spirit of self-sacrifice in the face of extreme peril sustains and enhances the highest traditions of the United States Naval Service."

The three members of the ill-fated Apollo 13 mission are, from left to right, Jim Lovell, Ken Mattingly, and Fred Haise. Lovell was a 1952 graduate of the Naval Academy, Mattingly a 1958 graduate of Auburn University, and Fred Haise a 1959 graduate of the University of Oklahoma. Lovell was honored as a distinguished graduate by the Naval Academy Alumni Association in 2001.

This photograph of Lawson P. Ramage was taken shortly after he was awarded the Medal of Honor by Pres. Franklin Roosevelt. He received the honor for "conspicuous gallantry" while serving as commanding officer of USS *Parche* during a predawn attack on a Japanese convoy off Takao, Taiwan, on July 31, 1944.

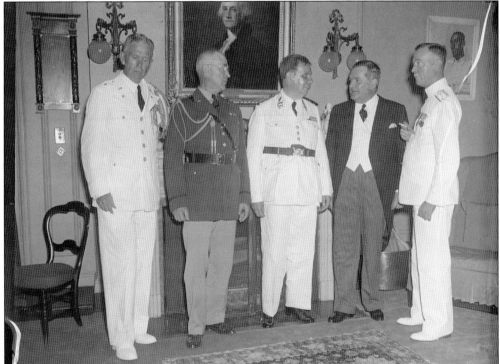

Gen. Goes Montero is entertained by Brig. Gen. George C. Marshall, US chief of staff Malin Craig, Brazilian ambassador Carlos Martins, and Adm. Wilson Brown, superintendent of the US Naval Academy, in 1939. Shortly before this reception, General Montero participated in a pass and review of the Brigade of Midshipmen.

Several members of the United Nations military staff receive a personal tour of the Naval Academy from Rear Adm. James L. Holloway Jr., superintendent. Although the photograph is undated, Admiral Holloway was superintendent from January 1947 to April 1950.

Adm. David F. Sellers bids Pres. Franklin D. Roosevelt farewell at the US Naval Academy around 1934-1938. Also pictured are, from left to right, Eleanor Roosevelt, Betsey Roosevelt, James Roosevelt, and Edmund W. Starling, presidential guard. Admiral Sellers was an 1894 graduate of the academy, the first from New Mexico. He served as superintendent from 1934 until his retirement in 1938.

The Navy receives the original commission of John Paul Jones in Washington, DC, in 1940. The document, dated October 10, 1776, commissioned Jones as a captain in the US Navy and was issued under the authority of the Continental Congress with the signature of John Hancock as its president.

Jones's commission was presented to Secretary of Navy Charles Edison by Capt. Harry A. Baldridge, US Navy (retired), curator of the US Naval Academy Museum. The commission was placed in the crypt of the Revolutionary War hero at the Naval Academy Chapel.

Pres. Herbert Hoover (center left) receives the class of 1881 and their spouses at the White House in 1929. Most of the men pictured saw service in World War I, including Adm. Henry Baird Wilson.

Pres. Warren G. Harding visits the Naval Academy and walks along a street next to the superintendent's residence, Buchanan House. The admiral walking beside the president is not identified, but it is likely Adm. Henry B. Wilson, the superintendent at the time. First Lady Florence Harding and a group of distinguished officers and guests were also present.

Pres. John F. Kennedy and Undersecretary of the Navy Paul B. "Red" Fay sit in a helicopter on the South Lawn of the White House en route to the commencement ceremony at the Naval Academy. In his commencement speech, Kennedy stated, "In my inaugural address, I said that each citizen should be concerned not with what his country can do for him, but what he can do for his country. What you have chosen to do for your country, by devoting your life to the service of our country, is the greatest contribution that any man could make."

James Stockdale graduated from the Naval Academy in 1946, but was part of the class of 1947 because of an accelerated wartime schedule. In 1965, his A-4 Skyhawk was shot down in North Vietnam. He was held a prisoner of war at the "Hanoi Hilton" until 1973. Stockdale was awarded the Medal of Honor in 1976, and retired a vice admiral in 1979. He is one of 73 USNA Medal of Honor recipients. The Vice Admiral James Stockdale Center for Ethical Leadership at the academy is named in his honor.

Vice Admiral Stockdale died of complications from Alzheimer's disease in 2005. Here, his flag-draped coffin is carried by an honor guard inside the Naval Academy Chapel. He is buried at the Naval Academy Cemetery.

Commander-in-chief of US Central Command Gen. Norman Schwarzkopf smiles as a member of the Naval Academy's class of 1991 raises his arms in exultation after receiving his diploma during the academy's graduation and commissioning ceremony at Navy–Marine Corps Stadium. Nearly 20,000 guests attended the ceremony, during which 937 midshipmen graduated. Just a few months prior to this ceremony, General Schwarzkopf led and helped quickly end the First Gulf War, also known as Operations Desert Shield and Storm. He retired from the military in August 1991.

David Robinson graduated from the Naval Academy in 1987 with a degree in mathematics. At seven feet, one inch tall, it would have been difficult for him to serve safely onboard any ships. He completed his five-year commitment to the Navy by serving on active duty as a civil engineering officer for two years and in the reserves for another three. He was drafted by the San Antonio Spurs in 1987, but did not start playing until 1989. Robinson is widely considered one of the greatest players in Naval Academy history.

Adm. Frank Kelso (USNA, 1952) takes the oath to assume the duties as the 24th chief of naval operations. He was a career submarine officer and took over the position from Adm. Charles Trost, also a Naval Academy graduate (1953). Admiral Kelso is a 2008 Naval Academy Alumni Association Distinguished Graduate.

Pres. Ronald Reagan addresses the graduating class of 1985. He was assisted by First Lady Nancy Reagan and Secretary of the Navy John Lehman. The ceremony was held at the Navy–Marine Corps Memorial Stadium. At the end of his address, Reagan stated, "Your countrymen have faith in you and expect you to make decisions. The issues will not be black and white; otherwise, there would be no decision to make. Do not be afraid to admit and consider your doubts, but don't be paralyzed by them. Be brave."

Pres. George W. Bush poses with the Naval Academy football team during the presentation of the Commander-in-Chief Trophy on the Rose Lawn on April 25, 2006. "Seniors on this team have led one of the most dramatic turnarounds in college football history," said the president. "The seniors are the sixth class in Academy history to have beaten Army all four years." The trophy is presented each year to the winner of the series between the US Military Academy Black Knights, Navy Midshipmen, and US Air Force Academy Falcons. The tradition began in 1951, and the Navy Midshipmen have won the trophy 16 times.

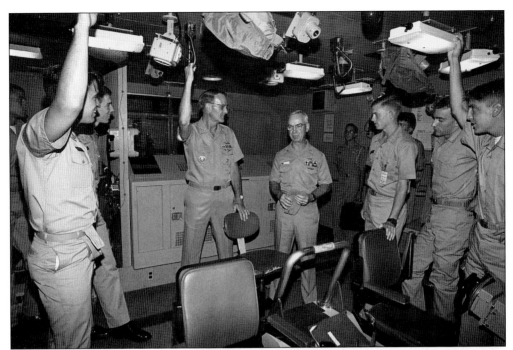

Rear Adm. Winford G. "Jerry" Ellis (USNA, 1964) provides a tour of a ballistic missile submarine to Adm. Charles Larson (USNA, 1958), superintendent of the Naval Academy, and a few midshipmen interested in pursuing a career in undersea warfare in the early 1990s. The handles overhead are used for support during deep-angle operations while underway. Before retiring from the Navy, Rear Admiral Ellis held the position of oceanographer of the Navy.

Elizabeth Rowe celebrates graduating from the US Naval Academy in May 1980, the first female graduate of the academy. Much like previous midshipmen who were "firsts," she endured hazing during her four years in Annapolis. Nevertheless, she endured and earned a degree in physics. She retired as a commander in 2000.

Adm. Michelle Howard is a 1982 graduate of the US Naval Academy and was the first African American woman to command a US Navy warship. She is the first female graduate of the Naval Academy to be selected for flag rank. Additionally, she was the first person selected from her class for flag rank, male or female. She is also the first female four-star admiral.

Designed by Park Benjamin, USNA 1867, the United States Naval Academy coat of arms, or seal, was officially adopted in 1899. The Latin inscription *Ex Scientia Tridens* translates to "From Knowledge, Seapower." The seal also includes a head-on view of an ancient ship, an open book, and a hand holding a trident.

DISCOVER THOUSANDS OF LOCAL HISTORY BOOKS FEATURING MILLIONS OF VINTAGE IMAGES

Arcadia Publishing, the leading local history publisher in the United States, is committed to making history accessible and meaningful through publishing books that celebrate and preserve the heritage of America's people and places.

Find more books like this at
www.arcadiapublishing.com

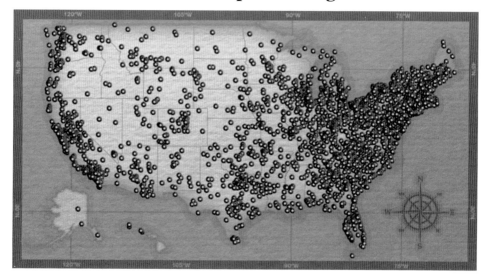

Search for your hometown history, your old stomping grounds, and even your favorite sports team.

Consistent with our mission to preserve history on a local level, this book was printed in South Carolina on American-made paper and manufactured entirely in the United States. Products carrying the accredited Forest Stewardship Council (FSC) label are printed on 100 percent FSC-certified paper.

MADE IN THE USA